I Am
Responsible

by Sarah L. Schuette

Consulting Editor: Gail Saunders-Smith, Ph.D.

Consultant: Madonna Murphy, Ph.D.
Professor of Education,
University of St. Francis, Joliet, Illinois
Author, *Character Education in America's
Blue Ribbon Schools*

Pebble Books

an imprint of Capstone Press
Mankato, Minnesota

Pebble Books are published by Capstone Press
151 Good Counsel Drive, P.O. Box 669, Mankato, Minnesota 56002
www.capstonepress.com

072010
5843VMI

Library of Congress Cataloging-in-Publication Data
Schuette, Sarah L., 1976–
    I am responsible / by Sarah L. Schuette.
    p. cm.—(Character values)
    Summary: Simple text and photographs show various ways children can
be responsible.
    Includes bibliographical references and index.
    ISBN-13: 978-0-7368-1443-0 (hardcover)
    ISBN-10: 0-7368-1443-4 (hardcover)
    ISBN-13: 978-1-4296-1566-2 (softcover pbk.)
    ISBN-10: 1-4296-1566-4 (softcover pbk.)
    1. Responsibility—Juvenile literature. 2. Children—Conduct of life—Juvenile
literature. [1. Responsibility.] I. Title. II. Series.
BJ1451 .S338 2003
179'.9—dc21   2002004286

Note to Parents and Teachers

The Character Values series supports national social studies
standards for units on citizenship. This book describes
responsibility and illustrates ways students can be responsible.
The images support early readers in understanding the text. The
repetition of words and phrases helps early readers learn new
words. This book also introduces early readers to subject-specific
vocabulary words, which are defined in the Words to Know section.
Early readers may need assistance to read some words and to use
the Table of Contents, Words to Know, Read More, Internet Sites,
and Index/Word List sections of the book.

Table of Contents

I am responsible. I do
what I should do.

I feed my goldfish.

8

I make my bed
every morning.

I brush my teeth.

I help my dad
dry the dishes.

I practice for
my piano lesson.

I get to
swimming lessons
on time.

I bring my supplies
to school.

People can depend on me. I am responsible.

Words to Know

depend—to count on someone to do the right thing

piano—a large musical instrument with white keys and black keys; people press the keys to make music on the piano.

practice—to work in order to learn a skill

responsible—doing what you say you will do; people who are responsible keep promises and follow rules.

supplies—materials needed to do something; school supplies include notebooks, pencils, and crayons.

Read More

Nelson, Robin. *Being Responsible.* First Step Nonfiction. Minneapolis: Lerner, 2003.

Raatma, Lucia. *Responsibility.* Character Education. Mankato, Minn.: Bridgestone Books, 2000.

Salzmann, Mary Elizabeth. *I Am Responsible.* Edina, Minn., Abdo Publishing, 2002.

Internet Sites

FactHound offers a safe, fun way to find Internet sites related to this book.

Go to *www.facthound.com*

FactHound will fetch the best sites for you!

23

Index/Word List

Word Count: 57
Early-Intervention Level: 8

Credits

Mari C. Schuh, editor; Jennifer Schonborn, series designer and illustrator; Gary Sundermeyer, photographer; Nancy White, photo stylist

Pebble Books thanks the Mankato Family YMCA of Mankato, Minnesota, and the Bacon family of North Mankato, Minnesota, for their assistance with this book.

The author dedicates this book to her grandmother, Minnie L. Simcox, of Belle Plaine, Minnesota.